AL QAIDA AND YEMEN – IS OUR CURRENT POLICY GOOD ENOUGH?

Al-Qaida in Yemen commonly referred to as Al-Qaida in the Arabian Peninsula (AQAP) threatens the United States and its citizens abroad. The U.S. takes this threat very seriously. However, national and diplomatic values closely held by the United States and other nation-states hinder a direct response to this lethal threat. Currently, AQAP members physically reside and enjoy "sanctuary" or "safe haven" within the sovereign borders of another nation, the Republic of Yemen. The people and the formal government of the Republic of Yemen suffer significant problems of their own and the uninvited presence of AQAP members represents the least of them. This critical fact presents the United States and its closest ally, the United Kingdom, with a significant dilemma; how can a nation-state eliminate the threat posed by AQAP members when AQAP leverages physical, informational, and spiritual sanctuary within the borders of another sovereign nation? This dilemma represents a significant challenge for first world nation-states threatened by non-state actors such as Al-Qaida's Yemen-based wing. By applying traditional nation-state-to-nation-state engagement rules, the United States and the United Kingdom must cultivate a key relationship with the Republic of Yemen in order to eliminate AQAP's sanctuary. Is the traditional nation-state response timely enough to address the threat posed by AQAP? After all, might a decade of spectacular attempted terrorist attacks against the United States and its interests by Al-Qaida's Yemen-based wing, such as the recent discovery of a bomb expertly hidden inside of an ink cartridge and flown on a United Parcel Service (UPS) aircraft, demonstrate the need to analyze, review, and perhaps modify the current strategic policies towards the Republic of Yemen.

The United States has been targeted by AQAP four times in the last year alone. The first attack occurred in November 2009, at Fort Hood, carried out by Army Major Nidal Hasan who reportedly received his inspiration, and education through the online teaching of American born Anwar al-Awlaki. A recent article suggests that Major Hasan exchanged at least 18 emails with al-Awlaki.[1] The second planned attack was the attempted bombing of NWA flight 253, on Christmas Day, carried out by Umar Farouk Abdulmutallab. The third planned attack was the Times Square car bomb attempt, carried out by Faisal Shahzad; and finally the recent attempted UPS cargo plane attack.

Al-Qaida's Yemen-based wing is part of the larger group now called al-Qaida in the Arabian Peninsula (AQAP), formed in January 2009, following a merger between al-Qaida groups in Yemen and Saudi Arabia to create a regional affiliate with dual-nationality leadership. All of the preceding attacks have been linked back to AQAP and a United States born Muslim cleric, Anwar al-Awlaki, an infamous character in the halls of the Federal Bureau of Investigation (F.B.I.) and the first American on the CIA's kill or capture list.[2] Anwar al-Awlaki provides input to potential terrorists as a master strategist, propagandist, and is an internet theological advisor for those who want to attack the United States. Another American in Yemen, Samir Khan, who has declared himself a traitor to the United States, is assisting in producing AQAP propaganda.[3]

AQAP uses the internet to reach out from Yemen to inspire, direct, and educate unstable, vulnerable individuals and convince them to perform terrorist acts against the United States. In all of these cases, AQAP either provided training, explosives, anti-U.S. propaganda, internet lectures, or cultural guidance in order to influence recruits to perform these illegal activities against the United States. Historically speaking, the

United States has been dealing with other al-Qaida attacks before the rise of AQAP to include the "Fort Dix Six" terrorist ring that was broken up by the F.B.I. in 2007. This group of westernized Albanian Muslims, inspired by the online teachings of Anwar al-Awlaki, planned to attack Joint U.S. Air Force Base McGuire and U.S. Army Base Fort Dix. Additionally, a shocking attack by Al Qaida against the USS Cole docked in the Port of Aden, in October 2000, killed 17 sailors. American military personnel were attacked at a hotel in Aden, while waiting to deploy to Somalia in support of the United Nations food relief operation in 1992.[4]

Not only has the United States been targeted by AQAP in the past year, but our closest ally and supporter for a stable and democratic Yemen, the United Kingdom, has also come under attack from AQAP. In early October 2010, the United Kingdom's Ambassador to Yemen was attacked by AQAP militants who "fired a rocket-propelled grenade at a British embassy car, slightly injuring one staff member as well as bystanders."[5] This attack forced the United Kingdom's Embassy to withdraw many of its staff in order to assess the potential safety risks. The security situation in Yemen jeopardizes both current and future assistance the United Kingdom's government is willing to provide to Yemen and its citizens. The worst case scenario is the security situation forces other nation-states and friends of Yemen to withdrawal their financial and international support. The United Kingdom's desire for Yemen is articulated by The Rt Hon Alan Duncan MP, Minister of State for the International Development UK. He states, "The challenge for all of us is to make sure we step up to the mark – the Government of Yemen, NGOs, the U.S., donors, Yemen's neighbors and the rest of the international community – and work together to bring peace and stability to ordinary Yemenis."[6]

In order to comprehend the complexity of the United States policy towards Yemen, it is important to understand some of the historical and cultural facts of Yemen. In turn, this background information highlights the current, critical, and wicked issues faced by the Government of Yemen everyday. The enormous challenges faced by the Government of Yemen are compounded by the presence and activities of al-Qaida in the Arabian Peninsula. AQAP is responsible for orchestrating attacks against the United States, against the Government of Yemen, on United Kingdom citizens working in Yemen and many other foreigners working or visiting Yemen. Several recommendations and suggestions will be made on strategic policy changes that may be used to further alleviate the threat from al-Qaida in the Arabian Peninsula. The question for the United States is "whether it can afford to wait for the Government of Yemen to disrupt the AQAP forces" and "can they do this effectively and quickly enough to prevent further, potentially catastrophic, acts of terrorism?" In order to understand the challenges the United States faces with regard to the current strategic policy towards Yemen, everyone must understand the complicated and challenging political, economic, and governance issues faced by the Government of Yemen.

Internal Warring Factions in Yemen

The political situation is tenuous at best for President Ali Abdallah Saleh, the Yemeni President since unification of North (Sana'a) and South (Aden) Yemen in 1990. North Yemen formally known as the Yemen Arab Republic or the "'republican'" north reflected a strong tradition of military authoritarianism, nationalism, and Islamism. Saleh assumed the Presidency of the Yemen Arab Republic through a military coup in 1978.

The two Yemen's merged into one state when the Soviet Union collapsed and with it the Marxist south lost its international partner and financial supporter. There are two principal Islamic religious groups in Yemen. The first Islamic religious group is the Yemeni Zaydi Shia which is one of the three Shia branches found mainly in North Yemen. The second Islamic religious group is the Shafa'I school of Sunni Muslims found in the Southern and Southwestern part of Yemen. The Zaydi Shia is the Shia faction that is closest to Sunni Islam. By percents there are about 40% Zaydi Shia and 60% Sunni in Yemen.[7] President Saleh is a member of the Sanhan tribe and a Zaydi Shia.

The elimination of internal conflict in the northern and the southern most regions of Yemen represent President Saleh's top priority. The fighting in the Northern Province has been very lengthy and costly. In fact, the recent negotiated peace brings to an end "the sixth bout of fighting in a cyclical six-year conflict. According to one estimate, the war was costing Sana'a up to $10 million dollars a day."[8] The northern Houthi Shia (part of the minority Zaydi Shia sect) rebellion is characterized by protests against the Saleh-led government and its alliance with US "friendly" initiatives. It is led by Hussein al-Houthi, a former parliamentary figure that parted with the Saleh regime in the 1990's to protest increasing Sunni radicalism from al-Qaeda and Wahhabi teachings. Interestingly enough, this is the same radical group the United States and its coalition partners are fighting all over the world. Saleh relies on aid from Saudi Arabia's military to control the uprising and some feel that the Houthi uprising has become a proxy war between Saudi Arabia and Iran played out on Yemeni soil.[9] Saleh describes the Northern Shia movement as pro-Iranian and seditious.[10]

The south, formerly known as the People's Republic of South Yemen(1967) and then as the People's Democratic Republic of Yemen (1970), by comparison was a patron of the Soviet Union since 1970, and can be characterized by socialism, Marxist beliefs, and Marxist practices.[11] The separatists feel that they were forced to join with the republican north in 1990 and that the north is occupying their state. Additionally, they protest the strong family-led Saleh government. In 2009, Tariq al-Fadhli, a southern jihadist, left the Saleh regime to become the leader of the southern movement. Saleh, in the past, has been known to use some of the jihadist's theologies that seem to sweep through Yemen to help his cause and keep factions under control "enlisting Sunni radical groups to fight what he has described as a pro-Iranian 'Shia' movement in the north and radical Salafi Islamists to fight the formerly Marxist forces in the south."[12] However, these groups seem to be coalescing into a more united front against the Saleh regime as the domestic situation remains tenuous and the population's basic needs continue to go unmet.

The ongoing cost of fighting the rebels has been a crippling financial burden on the Saleh government draining huge amounts of money and keeping the focus of his government on military spending versus providing basic services for its people. Recently Yemen asked the United States for more aid (dollars and training) to fight terrorism; however, there is concern that the Saleh government will not use the aid to fight AQAP as the United States intended.[13] President Saleh's regime has long been characterized by endemic corruption which is all too common in most government agencies, programs, and military leadership, further impeding the Government of Yemen's desire and drive to remove AQAP from their country.[14] Due to the close military ties to all of the immediate family members and their desire to stay in power, critics inside the Government of Yemen and within the United States have suggested that the aid could end up going to fight government opponents, either the Shia in the North or the secessionist in the south, instead of pursuing AQAP and its leadership.[15]

A Fractured Economy

Aside from internal unrest, another huge concern of the Yemeni government is its fractured economy. Like other states at risk, Yemen's population is large, young, poor, unemployed, poorly educated, and becoming more and more Islamized.[16] A high unemployment rate around 35%, low literacy rate of 50% which breaks down further as 70% for men and 30% for women, coupled with a large "youth bulge" where one third of the population is between the ages of 15 and 29 make youth unemployment a major problem.[17] Some reports have established the youth unemployment rate at almost double the adult rate making the youth rate around 70%. Over half of the population lives below the poverty line making Yemen the poorest country in the Arab world. With a per capita income of $930.00, Yemen ranks 166th out of 174 poorest countries worldwide.[18] Furthermore, the low per capita income and widespread poverty hamper the government's ability to tax business or individual incomes thus limiting the amount of capital available to invest in developing health and human service capacities. Lastly, the Yemeni population has almost doubled since 1990 and is set to almost double again by 2025 to almost 38 million people.[19] The population is growing at an unsustainable rate of 3.2 percent per year, adding more stress on the government's limited resources. All of these factors contribute to the Yemeni youth's susceptibility to AQAP's extremist messages.[20]

Another major economic issue facing the Yemeni government is the rapid decrease of oil production which leads to decreasing revenue earned from oil sold on the international market. In the next twenty years or so, experts are predicting that Yemen will run out of oil. Their 2009 oil receipts were nearly 60% less than the previous year curtailing the Government of Yemen's main source of revenue. [21]

A final major issue that limits economic growth is the lack of safe water resources. Current water supplies are rapidly decreasing thus contributing to waterborne diseases such as cholera and bacterial dysentery. In fact, waterborne diseases help to contribute to 70% of Yemen's incredibly high infant mortality rate.[22] The United States Agency for International Development proposed an aggressive program to assist with the water supply issue by teaching water conservation techniques, reducing soil erosion, restoring traditional terrace cultivation, and discouraging Qat production across the country.[23] One of the biggest users of water in Yemen is the Qat growing community.[24] Qat production and sales is a highly lucrative industry; however, the crop does not provide a food source for the country and the trees consume vast quantities of water.[25] The Government of Yemen in conjunction with USAID is actively campaigning to reduce the number of Qat trees. In fact, the Government of Yemen is encouraging the planting of almonds and coffee as an alternative cash crop. Further, the Government of Yemen is encouraging the growth of corn, wheat, and beans as a food crop. By encouraging farmers to remove Qat trees and plant other crops, the Government of Yemen achieves several goals to include water conservation, reducing the amount of Qat for use by Yemeni's, and it provides a sorely needed food crop for the people of Yemen. In summary, all of these real and current issues contribute heavily to the country's many economic, social, and governance concerns.

Military Defenses, Police, and Coast Guard

The Yemeni military (Army, Air Force, Navy, and Coast Guard) is the second largest on the Arabian Peninsula estimated at nearly half a million, second only to Saudi Arabia, with the bulk of the forces in the Army.[26] Thus the Yemeni military represents 2.1% of the total population of 23.8 million. In 2007, the Yemeni government reinstated the draft to help counter unemployment thus rapidly expanding the military ranks. The Yemeni military is led by the supreme commander of the armed forces Field Marshal Ali Abdullah Saleh, also the President of Yemen. Leadership within the military is dominated by members of President Saleh's family to include his son Ahmad who heads the Republican Guard and Special Forces. President Saleh's three nephews Amar, Yahya, and Tarek hold key national security positions including control of the elite Presidential Guard.[27] Additionally, President Saleh's half brother Muhammad Saleh al-Ahmar is Chief of the Air Force.[28] Clearly President Saleh retains tight control over the Yemeni military forces through his family members adding credence to the claims of nepotism and corruption within his regime.

In general, the Yemeni military equipment is considered to be light, outdated, and poorly maintained.[29] In an effort to offset the equipment challenges, the United States provided military equipment, training, and technical support through the International Military Education and Training (IMET) assistance program.[30] This support of the military is a reflection upon the earlier policies recognizing the importance of a strong Yemeni military with a capability to conduct counter-terror operations. The Yemeni Coast Guard was founded after the bombing of the USS Cole in 2000. The United States military has helped Yemen build and equip a modern Coast Guard along with continued training assistance. One of the important tasks of the Yemeni Coast Guard is to guard the strategically important Bab al Mandab strait where the Red Sea meets the Gulf of Aden and the Indian Ocean.[31] Both the United States and the United Kingdom provide military training assistance and logistical support to the Yemeni Special Operation Forces and other counter-terrorism units. The training includes military mission planning and tactical level unit instruction.[32] The United States recently committed 250 million dollars in military aid to the Government of Yemen for fiscal year 2011 thus doubling the amount of military aid from the previous year.[33] The Department of State provides additional training and capacity building programs for Yemeni law enforcement in an effort to counter the challenges the Yemeni police force faces with limited training, equipment, and professionalism.[34] In spite of the Yemeni Army's challenges, the Government of Yemen realizes the threat emanating from AQAP and continues to conduct military operations designed to disrupt AQAP's operational planning and deprive its leadership of a safe haven within the borders of Yemen. To date AQAP is able to live, plan, and recruit within the large, ungoverned spaces found throughout Yemen. These security operations may, over time, weaken and stress AQAP's leadership, thus denying AQAP the time and space it needs to plan, organize, and train for operations.[35]

Policy Goals for Yemen

In her recent travels to Yemen, Secretary of State Hillary Clinton further emphasized the Obama administration's position on the future of Yemen. "We seek a unified, stable, democratic and prosperous Yemen where civil society has room to operate but al-Qaida does not."[36] The Obama Administration is focused on a new, "whole of government" approach to Yemen that aims to mobilize and coordinate with other international actors. The new policy will address not only security and counterterrorism concerns but also the root causes of the instability. It aims to encourage political reconciliation, improve governance, and build the capacity of the Yemeni government to exercise authority and to address the economic and social challenges of delivering basic services to its people.[37] The current administration's efforts to focus on the economic, political, and social issues is an important part of the long term strategic policy. The existing counter-terrorism policy will continue to assist the Government of Yemen in their efforts to marginalize and limit the capabilities of AQAP. This policy is admittedly broad but meant to be flexible enough to adapt to changing needs encountered over time.

Detailed United States Strategic Policy

The detailed United States strategic policy towards Yemen is a two pronged process. The first priority is to strengthen the Government of Yemen's ability to secure and minimize the threat from violent extremists with its borders. The second and even more challenging priority is to mitigate the economic crisis and the deficiencies in the Government of Yemen's capacity to provide basic services, transparency, and adherence to the rule of law.[38] As stated earlier, the Department of State and Department of Defense is currently providing training and assistance to Yemen's key counterterrorism units within the Yemeni police and military forces to support efforts to fight terrorism. USAID has a new strategy of partnering with Yemen, focusing their efforts on increasing youth employment and other economic opportunities; improving the government's ability to deliver services in education and health care; working towards a transparent, decentralized government; reviewing and beginning agricultural programs; and, lastly, empowering youth, women and other marginalized groups.[39] The

11

United States Strategic Policy in Yemen for areas of development other than security is highly dependent on USAID initiatives; however, the United States is also working with the United Kingdom to support their efforts to provide stability in Yemen. The United Kingdom's strategy "identifies the urgent need to improve public-service delivery and strengthen state institutions. The policy is framed on the basis that prevention is better than cure."[40] The United Kingdom's strategic policy is synchronized with the United States strategic policy and has been for the last decade.[41]

In January 2010, the United Kingdom sponsored an international meeting focused on Yemen, where more than twenty countries signed up to a shared view and analysis of Yemen's issues. During this meeting, the Yemeni government brought a ten point plan that was brutally honest about the issues currently facing Yemen. The honest assessment was highly praised by both Secretary of State Hillary Clinton and British Foreign Secretary David Miliband. Both agreed that now Yemen would need to begin addressing the issues brought forward notably corruption and poor governance.[42]

One other major note from the initial meeting was the creation of the "Friends of Yemen" consisting of an informal network that "reflects an attempt to treat fragility as a process, not a series of events, and amounts to a mechanism for sustained engagement to keep the process going."[43] The United States joined the Friends of Yemen international group and supports their efforts to work with the Government of Yemen. The Friends of Yemen are focused on four major areas. The first one is support of a political National Dialogue and parliamentary elections in 2011. The second is a plan for new courts, an increase in police, and a judicial process program for remote areas. The third focus area is the preparation of a de-radicalization action plan. The last focus area is a renewed push for coordination and improvements in border security.[44]

The Friends of Yemen also announced two technical working groups offering assistance to the Government of Yemen on both the economy and governance led by the United Arab Emirates and Germany. The second working group will offer technical assistance on the rule of law and justice led by the Dutch and Jordanians.[45] In conjunction with this initiative, there is heavy emphasis on regional engagement by members of the Gulf Co-operation Council (GCC). The Friends of Yemen believe it is in the best interest of the GCC to engage in the issues of Yemen now because Yemeni issues will affect all of the surrounding Gulf countries. The worst case for the GCC is Yemen transitioning into a failed state status which could lead to instability spreading to these neighboring countries. Therefore, it would be in the GCC's best interest to assist Yemen in its post-oil transition economy. Most importantly, the GCC's aid presents a non-Western face and there is a strong preference for development assistance to come from Gulf, Arab, and Islamic countries.[46] The economic, governance, counterterrorism, and cumulative "other" support offered to Yemen is badly needed in both the short and long term. The concern about these proposals is the lack of initiative to deal with the immediate threat emanating from AQAP. Tough action now by the Government of Yemen and the United States should be equally emphasized as AQAP destabilizes Yemen, the surrounding countries, and the world.

Recommended Modifications to Current Strategic Plan

The Obama Administration's new strategic policy approach is one that will take time to produce results. The establishment of the new priorities and mobilization of the different interagency players is a slow and deliberate process. In the meantime, AQAP

13

will continue to thrive in the ungoverned spaces of Yemen planning and plotting against the United States and the United Kingdom. Perhaps the immediate strategic policy the United States needs to focus on is the severe degradation of AQAP's offensive capabilities, the elimination of AQAP's leadership, the discredidation of the AQAP organization, and the capture of the United States born cleric Anwar al-Awlaki. As eluded to earlier, al-Awlaki, born in New Mexico, "is the evil genius behind AQAP's English-language web journal *Inspire*, whose two publications so far have been a how-to-kill handbook for aspiring terrorists."[47] Anwar al-Awlaki is a master at using the internet to provide and promulgate his message of hate and contempt toward the United States as illustrated by his online lecture series aptly named "Constants on the Path of Jihad."[48] Excerpts from this website include teachings where he purports that Jihad does not depend on any particular land but that it is global without borders or barriers to stop it.[49] In essence, al-Awlaki is advocating that any person or group can be a go it alone or "lone wolf" terrorist simply by following his online readings and instructions easily found on the internet. In addition to the attacks this past year, the "Fort Dix Six" plotters of 2007 were westernized Albanian Muslims who used al-Awlaki's online lecture series for inspiration and theological direction to plan their attacks on the combined Air Force/Army Post at Fort Dix, New Jersey. Eljivir Duka, one of the convicted conspirators "repeatedly instructed other 'recruits' to download copies of Anwar al-Awlaki's lectures."[50] Duka stated, "It's called the 'Constants of Jihad, and this, ever since I heard this lecture brother I want everyone to hear it…this lecture is very necessary for people today."[51] Anwar al-Awlaki is well aware of how American society works to include knowledge of the United States and the United Kingdom's holiday routines, the large crowds that gather for sporting events and other cultural celebrations when U.S. citizens are especially vulnerable. It is clearly evident why the head of the National Counterterrorism Center, Michael Leiter, recently stated "I actually consider Al-Qaeda in the Arabian Peninsula with Al-Awlaki as a leader within that organization probably the most significant risk to the United States homeland."[52]

Training and Cooperation with Government of Yemen Military and Police

Understanding that cooperation with the Yemeni government is paramount, the United States must work within a delicate political balance of having few "boots on the ground" and keeping a "Yemeni face" on the elimination of AQAP. United States Special Operation Forces are training the Yemeni Special Forces in an effort to increase the tactical level skills needed to combat AQAP fighters. Once properly trained and tactically sound, these forces may be considered ready to locate, capture, or disrupt the AQAP leadership. In addition to the United States and United Kingdom's military elements of national power, all other elements of national power should be seriously considered in order to intensify and increase the training and aid to the Yemeni counter-terrorism units. In conjunction with the increased training of Yemeni forces, perhaps the United States or United Kingdom governments might be willing to utilize specially trained teams to assist Yemeni forces in locating and removing the leadership of AQAP. Of particularly interest to the United States is Anwar al-Awlaki, Nasir al-Washishi and "the clever bomb maker Ibrahim Hassan Al Asiri."[53] Locating and removing these individuals may potentially marginalize the organization and leadership of this powerful and dangerous group. The United States Government, with quiet consent and support from the Government of Yemen, should freely and aggressively use drones, as it does in Pakistan and as it did previously in Yemen, to assist in the elimination of the AQAP network and its leadership.

Economic Opportunity for All of Yemen

A secure environment encourages international companies to invest in foreign industries such as oil or gas exploration and recovery. Yemen has been working with multiple international companies (Korea Gas Corp, Swiss GDF Suez Company, and Total-a large United Kingdom Corporation) to develop its Liquid Natural Gas export capability. Yemen has about 16.9 trillion cubic feet of proven natural gas reserves that once fully explored and capitalized may be used to offset the falling oil reserves. In fact, by 2011, the projection is for Yemen's Liquid Natural Gas export capability to reach full capacity exporting close to 6.7 million metric tons of Liquid Natural Gas.[54] This opportunity may be fully capitalized on by the Government of Yemen to offset the loss of oil revenues. By doing so, the government is replacing one source of income native to Yemen (oil) with another native resource (natural gas). The Government of Yemen would be wise to use both of these native resources to combat the social and economic issues they identified to the Friends of Yemen group in 2010. By taking advantage of their ability to generate income from exporting both liquid natural gas and oil, and then using the income to support their people through public health and public services programs the Government of Yemen would prove with actions that it does care for its people. In addition, the ability to draw investors into its country is predicated on the safety and security found within Yemen and the government's ability to protect the areas where the gas companies and their employees are working. Businesses and donors alike are reluctant to provide assistance when airplanes and multiple industries are being threatened by AQAP.

Transparency with the Saleh Government

Once the income from the sale of liquid natural gas flows into the Government of Yemen it will be paramount for them to transparently invest these dollars into services for the people and the development of non-government businesses. The recent events in North Africa have impacted Yemen. So much so that President Saleh announced he will not seek re-election in 2013 nor will he hand over the presidency to his son.[55] In order to foster a positive transition following the election, the Saleh government has a prime opportunity to use the dual income provided by both natural gas and oil production to assist its citizens. This income has the economic potential to lower the unemployment rate, increase government services, and truly transform the government. There is even an opportunity to use the economic gain to bring the country together as one nation. The challenge for President Saleh is the fight against corruption, historically poor management of government funds, and charges of nepotism within the government leadership.

Strategic Message to the People of Yemen

The United States and the United Kingdom can provide assistance in crafting an aggressive strategic communication campaign in support of the Government of Yemen. The important question for the Saleh regime is transparency? In order for the strategic message to work the Saleh government must prove with action their seriousness in promoting a better life for their people. A strong and constant message needs to be shared with all the people of Yemen on how important it is economically and politically to rid the country of AQAP. The Gulf State governments, Arabic countries or otherwise, will be reluctant to invest in Yemen if AQAP is allowed to freely operate within the borders of Yemen. The long term economic, governance, and security plan should be

17

expressed to all of the Yemeni people so they can have some comprehension of just how many nations are willing, able, and ready to assist them. The strategic message certainly ought to have a Yemeni government face on it, spreading the word via newsprint, internet, radio, and any other media outlet available in Yemen.

The long range strategy for Yemen proposed by the current administration is admirable and has great promise, yet the U.S. cannot allow AQAP to continue to plan and execute attacks against the nation. John Brennan's (the White House's Chief Counterterrorism Advisor) recent comments echo the importance of quickly taking action against AQAP as he tells of AQAP attempting to "target food at hotels and restaurants inside the United States, perhaps slipping harmful agents into salad bars or buffets".[56] Agreeably the long range strategic plan of the United States, along with the long range strategic plan of the United Kingdom, the support of the Gulf Coast Countries, and other Arab countries is the strategic solution that prevents Yemen from becoming a failed state. However, it can be argued that there has to be an aggressive addition to our long and short range strategic foreign policy plan.

The U.S. should make weakening AQAP and its leadership its number one priority in Yemen. The United States, the United Kingdom, or the Gulf Coast Countries cannot wait for Yemen to find and remove AQAP. The constant threat AQAP poses to all nations of the world makes this effort the highest priority. The internal challenges faced by the Government of Yemen clearly limits their capabilities to locate, disrupt, and destroy AQAP on their own. The United States, with the support of the United Kingdom and the neighboring Arab nations must act now to eliminate and marginalize AQAP and capture or kill the AQAP leadership within the borders of Yemen. Once this is accomplished then the economic, governance, and military cooperation and assistance programs can really become the long range strategic focus. The U.S. should view Yemen as a strategic and lasting economic partner whose valued friendship is based on the idea of economic prosperity, good governance, military cooperation, safety, and security for all of its citizens.

Endnotes

[1] Catherine Herridge, "Awlaki Tops Bin Laden as Top Terror Threat To U.S., Counterterrorism Official Says," February 09, 2011, http://www.foxnews.com/us/2011/02/09awlaki-tops-bin-laden-terror-threat-counterterrorism.com (accessed February 9, 2011).

[2] Ibid.

[3] Eileen Sullivan and Matt Apuzzo, "Terror plot thwarted as US-bound explosives seized," The Washington Post, October 30, 2010, http://www.washingtpost.com/wp-dyn/content/article/2010/10/29/AR2010102903088_pf.html. (accessed October, 29 2010).

Herridge, "Awlaki Tops Bin Laden as Top Terror Threat To U.S., Counterterrorism Official Says"

FoxNews.com, "Yemen Wants More U.S. Military Aid to Fight Terrorism", November 9, 2010. http://www.foxnews.com/world/2010/11/09yemen-wants-military-aid-fight-terrorism, (accessed November 9, 2010).

[4] Jeffrey D. Feltman, "Yemen on the Brink: Implications for U.S. Policy", U.S. Department of State House Committee on Foreign Affairs, February 3, 2010. http://www.state.gov/p/nea/rls/rm136499.htm (accessed October 21, 2010).

[5] BBC News Middle East, "Twin attacks strike at Western targets in Yemen," BBC News, October 6, 2010. http://www.bbc.co.uk/news/world-asia-pacific-11482626. (accessed October 6, 2010).

[6] Alan Duncan, "Yemen: Political Dynamics and the International Policy Framework." Speech given by Minister of State for International Development. Chatham House: London, England (November 1, 2010), 6.

[7] Dr. Emile Nakhleh, Testimony on Yemen and Al-Qaida before the Senate Foreign Relations Committee, 20 January, 2010, 3-5.

[8] Ginny Hill, "What is Happening in Yemen?" Survival, March 25, 2010, 109.

[9] Nakhleh, Testimony on Yemen and Al-Qaida before the Senate Foreign Relations Committee, 5.

[10] Ibid, 5.

[11] Ibid, 5.

[12] Ibid, 5.

[13] FoxNews.com, "Yemen Wants More U.S. Military Aid to Fight Terrorism", November 9, 2010. http://www.foxnews.com/world/2010/11/09yemen-wants-military-aid-fight-terrorism (accessed November 9, 2010).

[14] Nakhleh, Testimony on Yemen and Al-Qaida before the Senate Foreign Relations Committee, 2.

[15] FoxNews.com, "Yemen Wants More U.S. Military Aid to Fight Terrorism", November 9, 2010. http://www.foxnews.com/world/2010/11/09yemen-wants-military-aid-fight-terrorism (accessed November 9, 2010).

[16] Nakhleh, Testimony on Yemen and Al-Qaida before the Senate Foreign Relations Committee, 3.

[17] Feltman, "Yemen on the Brink: Implications for U.S. Policy."

Nakhleh, Testimony on Yemen and Al-Qaida before the Senate Foreign Relations Committee, 3.

USAID YEMEN, "2010-2012 Yemen Country Strategy," 5. http://pdf.usaid.gov/pdf_docs/PDACP572.pdf

[18] Feltman, "Yemen on the Brink: Implications for U.S. Policy."

[19] Ibid.

[20] Ibid.

[21] Hill, "What is Happening in Yemen?" 108.

[22] USAID YEMEN, "2010-2012 Yemen Country Strategy," 4. http://pdf.usaid.gov/pdf_docs/PDACP572.pdf

[23] Ibid.

[24] Qat is an evergreen shrub of Arabia and Africa, the leaves of which are used as a narcotic when chewed or made into a beverage. Yemen Post English Newspaper Online-Media of the People, Official Authorities Seek to Eliminate Qat Trees, http://www.yemenpost.new/Detail123456789.aspx?ID=3&SubID=968 (accessed February 10, 2011).

[25] USAID YEMEN, "2010-2012 Yemen Country Strategy"4. http://pdf.usaid.gov/pdf_docs/PDACP572.pdf

[26] FoxNews.com, "Yemen Wants More U.S. Military Aid to Fight Terrorism", November 9, 2010. http://www.foxnews.com/world/2010/11/09yemen-wants-military-aid-fight-terrorism (accessed November 9, 2010).

[27] Nakhleh, Testimony on Yemen and Al-Qaida before the Senate Foreign Relations Committee, 2.

[28] Ibid, 2.

[29] GlobalSecurity.org, Yemen Military. http://www.globalsecurity.org/military/world/yemen/military-intr0.htm (accessed December 15, 2010).

[30] Ibid.

[31] Jeremy M. Sharp, "Yemen: Background and U.S. Relations," Congressional Research Services, July 7, 2009, 4.

[32] Jeffrey D. Feltman, "Yemen on the Brink: Implications for U.S. Policy."

[33] FoxNews.com, "Yemen Wants More U.S. Military Aid to Fight Terrorism", November 9, 2010. http://www.foxnews.com/world/2010/11/09yemen-wants-military-aid-fight-terrorism (accessed November 9, 2010).

[34] Jeffrey D. Feltman, "Yemen on the Brink: Implications for U.S. Policy."

[35] Hill, "What is Happening in Yemen?" 110.

[36] FoxNews.com, "Clinton in Yemen to press counterterror efforts", January 11, 2011. http://www.foxnews.com/world/2011/01/11/clinton-yemen-press-counterterror-efforts (accessed January 11, 2011).

[37] Feltman, "Yemen on the Brink: Implications for U.S. Policy.

[38] Ibid.

[39] Ibid.

[40] Hill, "What is Happening in Yemen?" 105.

[41] For example, the author, who was in Yemen in 2003 worked daily with our British counterparts supporting training and development of the Yemeni Special Police and Special Operation Force. The close relationship and support allowed the training teams a higher degree of success than would have otherwise been achieved.

[42] Jonathan Marcus, "Can Friends of Yemen bring about stability?",BBC News, January 28, 2010. http://news.bbc.co.uk/go/pr/fr-/2/hi/uk_news/politics/8484224.stm (accessed February 3, 2011).

Hill, "What is Happening in Yemen?" 106.

[43] Hill, "What is Happening in Yemen?" 106.

[44] Daniel Benjamin, "U.S. Counterterrorism Strategy in Yemen", U.S. Institute of Peace, September 8, 2010. http://www.state.gov/s/ct/rls/rm/2010/147296.htm (accessed October 20, 2010).

[45] Hill, "What is Happening in Yemen?" 106.

[46] Ibid, 106-107.

Sharp, "Yemen: Background and U.S. Relations", 13.

[47] Bruce Riedel, "The Brains Behind the Foiled Plane Plot", The Daily Beast, November 3, 2010. http://www.brookings.edu/opinions/2010/1030_al_qaeda_yemen_riedel.aspx?p=1 (accessed November 3, 2010).

[48] Evan Kohlman, "A Web of Lone Wolves," Foreign Policy, November 13, 2010. http://www.foreignpolicy.com/articles/2009/11/13/a_web_of_lone_wolves? (accessed November 12, 2010).

Riedel, "The Brains Behind the Foiled Plane Plot."

[49] Kohlman, "A Web of Lone Wolves."

[50] Ibid.

[51] Ibid.

[52] Herridge, "Awlaki Tops Bin Laden as Top Terror Threat To U.S., Counterterrorism Official Says."

[53] Riedel, "The Brains Behind the Foiled Plane Plot.

[54] U.S. Energy Information Administration, Independent Statistics and Analysis, Yemen December 8, 2010. http://www.eia.doe.gov/cabs/Yemen/NaturalGas.html (accessed December 8, 2010).

[55] Oliver Holmes, "Why Yemenis Doubt President Saleh's Offer to Step Down," February 3, 2011. http://news.yahoo.com/s/time/20110203/wl_time/08599204579200 (accessed February 2, 2011).

[56] Mike Levine, "AQAP Looking To Attack U.S. Food Supply?" December 21, 2010. http://liveshots.blogs.foxnews.com/2010/12/21aqap-looking-to-attack-u-s-food-supply/pr (accessed December 21, 2010).